Thomas Nield

The Temple Harp

Thomas Nield

The Temple Harp

ISBN/EAN: 9783337815370

Printed in Europe, USA, Canada, Australia, Japan

Cover: Foto ©Lupo / pixelio.de

More available books at **www.hansebooks.com**

THE TEMPLE HARP

BY REV. THOMAS NIELD.

AUTHOR OF

"Baptism in Short Meter,"

ETC., ETC.

FOR SALE BY THE AUTHOR,
ELMIRA, OTSEGO COUNTY, MICHIGAN.
PRICE 60 CENTS.

PREFACE.

In the following hymns the author's heart has broken its alabaster box of ointment, in the hope that its perfume may refresh other souls, by leading them nearer to God and heaven. In this hope he sends forth his little volume. It will be perceived that he is not an apostle of the "New Theology," which would heathenize the Old Testament, and so make Christ no longer "The Lamb of God which taketh away the sin of the world," but rather a philosophical gentleman of lofty ethical perceptions, having courage equal to his convictions; nor yet one who thinks it wrong to sing what it is right to talk in the Lord's house. In verse and prose, in song and prayer, in the closet and the temple, give us Jesus, in some aspect of his person, his teaching or his life; for where Jesus is not, God is afar off. But we demand Jesus the God-man; for where the God is not, only a man is left, and man is the equal of Christ. Let any one read the prophecies of the Old Testament, and the gospels of the New, and then say whether he dare make such claims for himself, or for any other man, as are there made for "the Christ, the Son of the living God." T. N.

TABLE OF CONTENTS.

	PAGE.
God Incomprehensible	13
The Triune God	14
What We Know of God	15
The Voice of God in His Works	16
Psalm I	17
Psalm II	18
Psalm III	19
Psalm V	20
Psalm LXXV	21
Psalm XC	22
Christ the First Fruits	23
Psalm XCIII	24
Psalm C	25
Psalm CIII	26
Psalm CXXX	27
Psalm CXXXIII	28
Psalm CXLVI	29
Psalm CL	30
Great Tidings of Great Joy	31
The Wondrous Birth	32

TABLE OF CONTENTS.

	PAGE.
The Word was God	33
The Lamb of God	34
He is Risen	35
Shall Man be Just with God?	36
The Rich Became Poor	37
The Way, the Truth, the Life	38
The True Rock	39
Christ with Us	40
The Altogether Lovely	41
The Conquering Kingdom	42
Thy Kingdom Come	43
The Gospel Triumphant	44
The Greater Miracles	45
The Holy Spirit's Work	46
God Found in His Work	47
The Holy Book	48
Love of the Word	49
God's Word Unchangeable	50
The Truth Abides	51
The Lord's Memorial Day	52
The Holy Day	53
Joy in Worship	54
In the Sanctuary	55

TABLE OF CONTENTS.

	PAGE.
Gethsemane	56
The Costly Sacrifice	57
An Advocate with the Father	58
Self-Denial	59
Consecration	60
Faith	61
Desire for Faith	62
Self-Righteousness Vain	63
Saved by Grace	64
Assurance	65
My Trust	66
Grace for Grace	67
Seeking Help	68
Free in Christ	69
Glorying in Christ	70
The Sinner's Friend	71
The Heavenly Bread	72
Buried with Christ	73
Bearing the Cross	74
Help Received	75
Pleasant Ways	76
Self Lost in God	77
God My Strength	78

TABLE OF CONTENTS.

PAGE.

Afflictions	79
The Cross Twice Borne	80
Loving the Savior	81
Trust in Christ	82
My Treasure	83
Divine Goodness	84
Prayer for Christlikeness	85
Prayer for Purity	86
A Desire to Depart	87
Jesus Precious in Death	88
Seeking the Spirit's Aid	89
Be Thankful	90
Be Not Anxious	91
Have Courage	92
Watch and Pray	93
Hold On	94
The Christian Race	95
A Friend in Need	96
Loss is Gain	97
Gone Home	98
Rejoice	99
Confession	100
Revive Us Again	101

	PAGE
Forgive as We Forgive	102
By the Rivers of Babylon	104
The Ways of Providence	105
Murmuring	106
We Know in Part	107
The New Jerusalem	108
Saved by Hope	109
In the Wilderness	110
The Glorious Hope	111
The Almighty Shepherd	112
Heaven	113
Our House Above	114
In Remembrance	115
Bearing Christ's Afflictions	116
A Temple of the Holy Spirit	117
Spiritual Communion	118
The Friend of the Poor	119
The Increase of God	120
Divine Knowledge	121
Stewardship	122
Using as Not Abusing	123
Worldly Cares	124
Children of a King	125

	PAGE.
God Will Provide	126
Be Not Fearful	127
Dismissing Care	128
Daily Victory	129
To-Morrow	130
Our Opportunity	131
My Mission	132
Do Thy Work	133
Why Stand Ye Idle?	134
The Sinner's Plea	135
Your Work	136
The World for Jesus	137
At the Mercy Seat	138
Pray On	139
The Hour of Prayer	140
Asking Amiss	141
The Faithful One	142
Brotherly Love	143
Man Immortal	144
The All-Seeing Eye	145
The Fool's Hope	146
Sowing and Reaping	147
The Downward Road	148

PAGE.

Divine Long-Suffering............ 149
Warning.................... 150
The Passover................ 151
Losing the Soul.............. 152
Delaying.................... 153
No Peace in Sin............. 154
Choose..................... 155
In the Storm................ 156
Repenting................... 157
Make a Stand for Jesus...... 158
The Reward of Sin is Sure... 159
The Judgment Day........... 160

ERRATA.

Page 43, line 6—for "bend" read "tend."
Page 47, line 10—read "unsealed."
Page 62, line 5—for "brace" read "trace."
Page 66, line 11—after "goodness" read "doth."
Page 76, line 9—for "much" read "such."
Page 104, line 1—for "Babylon's" read "Babylonia's."
Page 166, line 1—for "Lost" read "Tost."

GOD INCOMPREHENSIBLE.

Great Being! vainly finite thought
  Would try to grasp infinity.
In vain the greatest minds have sought,
  With all their powers, to fashion thee.

Beyond the farthest orb of light
  That greets the earth with glimmering rays,
Thou art as limitless in might
  As where on myriad worlds we gaze.

Whate'er exists thy hands have made;
  Its destiny thine eye hath scanned.
The future, to thy mind portrayed,
  Is only what that mind had planned.

In vain, then, would our finite thought
  Attempt to grasp infinity.
In vain the greatest minds have sought,
  In vain shall seek, to fashion thee.

THE TRIUNE GOD.

Eternal God! who madest known
Thyself at first upon thy throne,
    One God, and only one,—
We joy that, in a later day,
Thou show'dst us, in a gracious way,
    Thy Godhood in the Son.

We praise thee, too, that later still
Thou madest known thy fuller will
    As God the Comforter.
Thus Father, Son and Spirit blend,
And we are brought to apprehend
    Thy threefold character.

Grant, O Thou triune God, that we
That threefold character may see,
    And find a threefold grace.
Come, Jesus! wash away our sin;
Come, Spirit! sanctify within;
    Then, Father, show thy face.

WHAT WE KNOW OF GOD.

Lord, since we so little know
Of thy wondrous works below,
Vain indeed the task must be
When our minds would compass thee.

Yet how much of thee we know,
Mirrored in thy works below;
Much of mightiness to fear,
Much of wisdom to revere.

And thou dost the power bestow
Grandest things of thee to know;
Truths that else must lie concealed
In thy Word we find revealed.

There thou dost thy nature show
Till thy very heart we know,
And we smile to look above,
Knowing well that thou art Love.

THE VOICE OF GOD IN HIS WORKS.
Psalm xix. 1-3.

In awful vastness o'er our head
The heavens are like a curtain spread,
And through their realms conspicuous shine
Proofs that their Maker is divine.

The firmament, in various ways,
His wondrous handiwork displays,
And all its changing scenes proclaim
The glories of Jehovah's name.

With soundless eloquence the day
Tells of his universal sway,
And when the night in splendor glows
The presence of a God it shows.

And hence, where'er the wanderers be,
These silent witnesses they see,
And seem to hear an inward voice:
"Lo, God is here, let man rejoice."

PSALM I.

Blest is the man that heedeth not
    The counsel the ungodly give,
Nor with the sinner casts his lot,
    Nor lives as wicked scorners live.
The law of God is his delight,
    And in that law he meditates,
Makes it his guide by day and night,
    Content to do as it dictates.

He shall be like a thrifty tree
    Planted where streams perennial flow;
His fruit shall in its season be;
    His leafy years no withering know.
Prosperity shall mark his way;
    On all he does a blessing rest,
Brightening his life from day to day,
    And making him divinely blest.

Not so the godless: they are driven
    Like chaff from autumn's threshing floor.
When judgment is in justice given,
    They are undone forevermore;
For God, who knows his people's ways,
    With blessings will their steps attend,
But they who spurn him all their days
    Shall find at last a dreadful end.

PSALM II.

Why do the powers of earth combine
    To thwart the purposes of God?
In vain they brave the power divine,
    Which smites with an almighty rod

The Lord who sits enthroned on high
    Shall at their futile fury laugh,
Till at his whirlwind voice they fly
    As lightly as the empty chaff.

His will is earth's established law,
    The anchor of his firm decrees;
And he will unborn millions draw
    To own his Son on bended knees.

That Son, enthroned, shall claim his own;
    From east to west display his power;
His right through all the earth make known,
    And seize the nations as his dower.

Beware, ye kings and judges, lest
    Your opposition rouse his wrath;
To him be your desires addrest,
    Nor dare to tempt the power he hath.

PSALM III.

Many, Lord, against me rise,
To assail me with their lies,
Help, they say, is not for me,
Since I have no help in thee.

But thou art a shield of power,
Guarding me in danger's hour;
Source of joy when joy is fled,
Lifting up my drooping head.

Thou hast heard me in the past,
When on thee my care I cast;
Then I laid me down and slept
And awoke, in safety kept.

Why, then, should I fear to-day,
Though my foes are in array?
Save me, O my God, once more;
Bless me as thou hast before.

From thy throne of justice look;
Give to sin a strong rebuke.
Since salvation is thine own,
Graciously let it be shown.

PSALM V.

The wings of morn shall bear
To thee my song and prayer,
    My God and King.
While I am sinful dust,
Thou holy art and just,
Yet in thy name I trust,
    Whose praise I sing.

The wicked shall not stand,
But feel thy mighty hand
    In dread rebuke;
But as for me, my face
Is toward the holy place,
Whence, from a throne of grace,
    To thee I look.

When snares the wicked lay,
Be with me in the way,
    Lest I should yield.
Then shall my glad heart be
A harp of praise to thee,
While thou dost compass me
    As with a shield.

PSALM LXXV.

To thee, O God, our thanks we pay,
  Whose presence all thy works declare;
For though the earth should pass away,
  Thou still unmoved art reigning there.

Thy power can lay the people low;
  That power the solid earth sustains.
Let mortals, then, be wise to know
  How terrible is he who reigns.

Let pride be low at thy behest,
  Who settest up and puttest down;
For vain would south and east and west
  Exalt the man who has thy frown.

A cup of wrath is in thy hand,
  And nations drink it in the hour
When they across thy purpose stand,
  And think to thwart thy righteous power.

But we thy righteousness declare,
  And sing thy praises day by day,
Assured we shall thy favor share
  When wicked men are cast away.

PSALM XC.

Thou, Lord, hast shown thy people grace
    Through all the ages known;
Thou who before the earth had place
    Wert high upon thy throne.

The sweep of everlasting years
    That bear their myriads by,
To thee as yesterday appears,
    So swift the ages fly.

As on a flood, earth's millions pass
    To an eternal sea;
Or as a sleep, or as the grass,
    They all appear to thee.

Our secret sins, as in thy light,
    Have darkened all our days;
And we have felt thine anger smite
    Until we mourned our ways.

Oh, teach us so our days to count
    That we may wiser be,
And dedicate the whole amount
    In service unto thee.

Return, O Lord, in pitying love,
    With thy refreshing grace;
And while we turn our eyes above,
    Oh, let us see thy face.

CHRIST THE FIRST FRUITS.

Christ is risen from the dead,
    Therefore shall his people rise;
Rise to share with him, their Head,
    Endless glory in the skies.

Vain the powers of earth oppose;
    Vain the hosts of death and hell;
They shall rise as Jesus rose,
    In his might invincible.

Let us then exultant sing
    Of our Leader's power to save.
Death in him has lost its sting;
    Glory gleams beyond the grave.

PSALM XCIII.

The Lord is throned above the spheres,
    In majesty arrayed,
And there, through his eternal years,
    His might shall be displayed.

The everlasting God, he reigns,
    And shall forever reign;
The world's foundations he sustains,
    Who only can sustain.

The floods, which lift their awful forms,
    Display his dreadful power;
Earth hears his voice in thundering storms,
    And trembles in that hour.

Yet greater than the vastest sea,
    And mightier than the storm,
God still o'er all his works will be,
    Who gave them first their form.

But while his greatness fills with awe,
    His truth and grace combine
To make us love his holy law,
    Whose precepts are divine.

PSALM C.

Let every land extol the Lord
    And worship him alone,
The story of his love record
    In songs before his throne.

Our God, he made us and doth keep,
    As with a shepherd's care,
And for his people, as his sheep,
    A pasturage prepare.

Then let us, with a gladsome voice
    And thankful heart and mind,
Together in his courts rejoice;
    For he is good and kind.

His mercy like himself shall last,
    Nor ever know an end;
His truth, as through the ages past,
    To endless years descend.

PSALM CIII.

Bless thou the Lord, my soul, and let
   My grateful powers proclaim his praise.
Yea, bless the Lord; and ne'er forget
   What benefits enrich thy days.
For nought of good his hands refuse;
But he forgives thee, saves, renews.

As in the ancient days were shown
   His wondrous power and gracious will,
So by his people is he known
   As merciful and gracious still.
So slow to wrath, so quick to aid,
Our ill deserts he has not paid.

His mercy is as high as heaven,
   To such as bow at his behest;
The memory of their sins is driven
   Far as the east is from the west.
A father's pity thus he shows;
For he his children's weakness knows.

We are but as the grass or flower
   That falls before the passing gust;
It flourishes its little hour,
   Then withers back again to dust.
But with the Lord is mercy still,
For those who love and do his will.

PSALM CXXX.

Out of the depths to thee I cry;
    Lord, turn not thou away,
But let me find thee very nigh
    To answer while I pray.

Shouldst thou all secret thoughts record,
    And motions of the heart,
Oh, who could bear his just reward,
    Nor hear thee say, Depart?

But thy forgiveness is a fount
    Of never-failing grace,
To such as on thy mercy count,
    And humbly seek thy face.

Hence 'tis on thee my soul would wait,
    While weary, weak and worn,
As those who watch, with heart elate,
    To greet the blush of morn.

May all thy people join with me
    To fix their hopes above,
That all may thy salvation see,
    And prove thy gracious love.

PSALM CXXXIII.

Good and pleasant is the sight
When the sons of God unite;
Peace upon their souls is shed,
Like the oil on Aaron's head;
And the holy lives they live
A perfume of blessing give.

As refreshing is the sight
As the dew on Hermon's height;
Zion feels its gracious power,
Given as a heavenly shower,
Quickening all her hidden roots,
Bringing forth divinest fruits.

By the Spirit's power and light
Thus the sons of God unite;
And the good in them begun
Shall in streams of blessing run,
From the Spirit's boundless store,
Even life forevermore.

PSALM CXLVI.

Praise the Lord, ye people, praise!
With my soul your anthems raise.
I will praise him while I live,
And in death new praises give.

Let not princes have your trust,
Who are children of the dust;
Vainly is their favor earned,
When they have to dust returned.

Happy he whose hope relies
On the Lord of earth and skies;
By whose will all things exist;
On whose bounty they subsist.

While his power to help exceeds
All his helpless creatures' needs,
He beholds with pitying eye,
Marks the tear and hears the sigh.

Those who trust him, he will own,
When the wicked are o'erthrown;
For the Lord forever reigns,
Praise him then in joyful strains.

PSALM CL.

Here in his courts let saints rejoice,
And praise the Lord with cheerful voice;
While all the heavenly orbs declare
His greatness and his glory there.

Praise him for all his mighty deeds
Who knows so well his creatures' needs
And, knowing, every blessing grants,
To satisfy their daily wants.

Let highest notes of praise abound
On every instrument of sound,
Till an orchestral joy shall roll,
As poured from one exultant soul.

Let all that breathes unite to raise
A grateful anthem in his praise;
Sea, earth and heaven, with one accord,
Sing hallelujah to the Lord.

GLAD TIDINGS OF GREAT JOY.

Tell the tidings through the earth
Of the great Messiah's birth.
Laying by his diadem,
Christ is born in Bethlehem.

He in highest heaven was known,
Seated by his Father's throne;
Here, the rod of Jesse's stem,
Christ is born in Bethlehem.

He, the hope of all the years,
Now upon the earth appears;
In time's crown the brightest gem,
Christ is born in Bethlehem.

Waft the tidings far and wide,
Over every ocean tide.
Tell the nations that for them
Christ is born in Bethlehem.

THE WONDROUS BIRTH.

Oh, sing to-day, ye sons of earth,
　　As unto you we bring
The story of the Savior's birth
　　And crown him while ye sing.

With gladsome heart receive him now,
　　As Prophet, Priest and King;
Let all your powers before him bow,
　　And crown him while ye sing.

The choicest offerings of your love
　　In adoration bring,
And with the raptured hosts above,
　　Oh, crown him while ye sing.

Let all the corners of the earth
　　With halleluiahs ring,
To celebrate the wondrous birth,
　　And crown him while ye sing.

THE WORD WAS GOD.

In thee alone, incarnate Word,
    The mind of God has been exprest;
Yet not in speech that ears have heard
    Through thee our spirits are addrest.

The hidden truths that none could find
    Shone clearly in thy life below,
Illuminating every mind
    That would the mind eternal know.

The Infinite and finite thus
    Have an interpreter in thee,
Through whom the Godhead speaks to us,
    In whom his character we see.

Oh, give us ears that will to hear
    Thy message of eternal love,
And hearts that always feel thee near,
    Directing them to things above.

THE LAMB OF GOD.

O Lamb, by God provided
　　The world's great sin to bear,
To thee has been confided
　　A task that none may share.
All other sacrifices
　　But pointed on to thine,
Which in itself comprises
　　All blessing, since divine.

A lamb—thyself unsinning—
　　For sinners thou didst die,
That man from the beginning
　　Might on thy death rely.
And forth through future ages,
　　Whoever trusts in thee,
The Father's love engages
　　To set that sinner free.

This only Lamb is offered,
　　Who only can atone;
And life to us is proffered
　　Through him who gave his own.
O Christ! our sins confessing,
　　We trust thy dying love.
Now speak in us the blessing
　　Of pardon from above.

HE IS RISEN.

All hail the morn when Jesus rose
    Triumphant o'er the grave.
He who o'ercame the last of foes
    Can all his people save.

Lift up your heads, ye gates of light.
    And let the Conqueror in;
He who, omnipotent in might,
    Defied the hosts of sin.

Let saints and angels crown him now
    Who bore on earth our shame;
With fadeless honors deck his brow,
    And glorify his name.

Sweep all your golden harps above,
    Tune all your tongues below,
To magnify the matchless love
    That none can fully know.

SHALL MAN BE JUST WITH GOD?
Job ix. 2.

Lord, how shall man be just with thee,
Whose eye his inmost thoughts can see,
And mark the motions of his will,
So prone to play the part of ill?

Those thoughts have oft had taint of sin;
That will has oft rebellious been;
Thy gracious gifts have been abused;
Thy calls to duty oft refused.

And yet thy faultless law demands
A faultless service at our hands.
Then how shall man be just and live,
Who does not such a service give?

A faultless Substitute appears
And scatters all our sins and fears.
Through him eternal life we gain—
The sinless One for sinners slain.

THE RICH BECAME POOR.

II. Cor. viii. 9.

Behold the matchless grace
By our Redeemer shown,
That he should leave his place
Beside the Father's throne,
And stoop to wear our sinful frame,
To bear the burden of our shame.

From heaven his pity saw
The race of Adam lie,
Doomed by a righteous law,
Which sentenced it to die;
And then, unmindful of the loss,
He left the crown and took the cross.

The richest thus became
The poorest for our sake,
That, through his righteous name,
We might with him partake
The glory of the great reward,
As heirs together with our Lord.

THE WAY, THE TRUTH, THE LIFE.

John xiv. 6.

Thou art the Way, through whom alone
  A sinner may salvation find.
In vain they would approach the throne
  Who leave thy cleansing blood behind;
But all who to the Father flee
Are welcome when they go through thee.

Thou art the Truth, whose mission shows
  Our fallen, lost, and helpless state.
Thy sufferings, too, the fact disclose,
  That God is holy, just, and great.
As in a mirror, thus we see
The Father and ourselves in thee.

Thou art the Life, whose grace imparts
  A power that none besides can give:
The power to quicken sin-dead hearts,
  And make them in thine image live.
Then give thy life to us, that we
May be the sons of God in thee.

THE TRUE ROCK.
Matthew xvi. 16.

Oh, rock of truth, by man confest;
    "Thou art the Christ, the Son of God."
Upon this rock the storms we breast,
    As on our upward way we plod;
On this in buoyant life rely;
Here find support when called to die

In vain the forms that men devise;
    Their sacerdotal pomp and state;
The boast that they are godly-wise,
    And guardians of the glory-gate.
They use the senses as a lure,
And make the spirit's bondage sure.

Our hope of heaven must be from heaven;
    For only God to God can lead.
By him our sins must be forgiven,
    And he supply our daily need.
While nought of earth can aught avail,
The Christ of God can never fail.

CHRIST WITH US.

Matt. xxviii. 20.

Ascended Lord, we joy to know
That, as the ages come and go,
   Thou still art with thine own.
Enthroned above the earth's affairs,
Thy answers to thy people's prayers
   Make here thy presence known.

Along the centuries we can trace
The glorious victories of thy grace,
   When right has wrong restrained.
We see thy hand in every stroke
That's freed men from oppression's yoke
   Till truth and freedom reigned.

And still we see thee in the fight,
And feel thee make our weakness might,
   While still thy foes assail.
Oh! let the ages yet to be
More wondrously thy presence see,
   More gloriously prevail.

THE ALTOGETHER LOVELY.
Cant. ii. 1.

How lovely the Savior appears,
    How fragrant the sense of his love,
When, looking to him through our tears,
    His presence and favor we prove.
Where he is a Sharon we find,
    And he is its beautiful rose,
And over the spirit and mind
    An odor of pleasure he throws.

A lily in him we can see,
    That grew in this valley below,
Transplanted from heaven, that we
    Might somewhat of paradise know.
How humble the scene of his birth,
    And lowly his earthly career!
And purity more than of earth
    Was seen in his character here.

His favor is fair as a rose,
    A solace and comfort to saints;
It breathes a perfume on their woes,
    Composing their saddest complaints.
A lily that knoweth no stain,
    A pattern he is for the pure,
And all who his graces attain
    A share in his glory secure.

THE CONQUERING KINGDOM.

Psa. ii. 8.

Lord, we believe the promise true,
That thou wilt yet the world subdue,
And all the heathen nations bring
To own the Savior as their king.

Thy truth is conquering day by day,
And yet shall have a boundless sway,
And every error vanish hence
Before that truth's omnipotence.

Its course is ever on, though slow,
The ages brightening as they go;
And thou shalt yet all glory gain;
For Christ is King, and he must reign.

THY KINGDOM COME.

Matt. vi. 10.

Lord, let thy kingdom come, as thou
    Hast taught our lips to pray,
Till at thy feet the nations bow
    And own thy sovereign sway.

Thus far the footsteps of thy power
    Toward such a triumph bend.
Oh, hasten thou the happy hour
    That brings the glorious end!

Let error vanish like the night
    When glinting dawn appears;
Thy truth, as o'er the mountain height,
    Illuminate the years.

Bid every age, with brighter glow,
    Foregleam the reign of love,
When men shall do thy will below
    As angels do above.

THE GOSPEL TRIUMPHANT.

Thou with whom are all the ages,
    We perceive a rounded plan,
Shadowed forth on history's pages,
    For the lifting up of man.
Centuries of preparation
    For the coming of thy Son
Speak a far-off consummation,
    When redemption's work is done.

Continents and isles are waking,
    Startled into life and power;
Error's chains thy truth is breaking,
    Bringing freedom's blessed hour;
And a nearing of the nations
    Gives a sense of brotherhood,
Which shall make their emulations
    Efforts for a common good.

These we view as index fingers,
    Pointing toward the things to be;
And, howe'er we think he lingers,
    Man is drawing nearer thee.
May these signs our hearts embolden
    For the battle but begun,
Knowing that millenniums golden
    Wait the triumph of thy Son.

THE GREATER MIRACLES.

O Son of God, yet man with men !
    Nature obeyed thy mighty nod,
And owned thee God of nature when
    Thou didst the deeds of nature's God.

Mankind beheld those wondrous deeds
    Forthspringing from a fount of love;
For thou didst bring to human needs
    A Father's blessing from above.

And now, though man with men no more,
    To do the deeds the eye may scan,
Thou still art gracious as before,
    Performing deeds of good for man.

Yet not the outward deed is thine,
    To bless men in a sensuous way,
But with an inward power divine
    Thy miracles are wrought to-day.

The Spirit takes thy body's place,
    Performing wondrous works again;
The greater miracles of grace,
    Which bring to life the souls of men.

THE HOLY SPIRIT'S WORK.
Zech. iv. 6.

Man can not cleanse the sinful soul,
Nor bend the will to his control,
    By aught that he can do;
But still the heart will be defiled,
The will rebellious, wayward, wild,
    The evil to pursue.

No, not by might of human hosts,
Nor by the power that wisdom boasts,
    Are souls from evil won;
But by the Spirit's power within,
Which overcomes the love of sin,
    The saving work is done.

Then come, O Spirit, and impart
The saving power to every heart,
    And sanctify the will;
That Christ within our hearts may reign,
As Monarch o'er his own domain,
    His purpose to fulfill.

GOD FOUND IN HIS WORD.

Lord, when thy vastest works we view,
    Then turn the least to note—
Whether above us in the blue
    Or in a living mote—
We can not tell which most displays
    The greatness of thy mind;
Yet in thy works, where'er we gaze,
    Thyself we can not find.

'Tis in thy written Word alone
    Thy secrets are revealed;
There all thy character is shown,
    Through holy men revealed.
That Word we gladly make our choice,
    Consulting it with care;
We hear its precepts as thy voice,
    For thou, O God, art there.

THE HOLY BOOK.

Book of books, whose blessed pages
    Mirror forth the mind of God!
In thy light the ancient sages
    From the glooms of error trod;
And the millions of the ages
    Up to higher levels plod,
In the pathway of thy pages,
    Leading upward unto God.

Fount of truth, forever flowing
    For the thirsty souls of men,
Life on those who drink bestowing,
    Bring, oh, bring the era when,
Wider still and farther going,
    Eden shall return again,
As the music of thy flowing
    Tells of peace, good will to men.

LOVE OF THE WORD.

O Lord, I love thy law;
   'Tis daily my delight;
For wisdom thence I draw,
   To guide my feet aright.
Without it I must go astray,
Nor even know the narrow way.

For what are human rules,
   In human weakness made?
The guesses of the schools,
   Where learning is displayed?
They all are foolishness to thee,
And an uncertain maze to me.

But thou, who madest heaven
   And earth, and all that is,
A faultless law hast given;
   And he who follows this
Shall never find his feet astray,
With such a lamp to light his way.

GOD'S WORD UNCHANGEABLE.

The works, and ways, and thoughts of man
    Are changeful as the billowy sea;
But Truth has never changed, nor can,
    But has eternal fixity.

Like God, the Truth was never young;
    Like him, it never can be old.
It was ere earth in ether swung,
    And will be when her knell is tolled.

Hence why the Word of God abides,
    Unchanged 'mid every flux of time;
Since in that Word the truth resides,
    As 'twere in youth's perpetual prime.

Then vainly men their progress boast,
    And test the Word by human sense;
Their progress indicates, at most,
    The changes in their ignorance.

Let all the storms of error rage;
    Let others drift on shoreless seas;
That word I make my anchorage,
    And in the harbor ride at ease.

THE TRUTH ABIDES.

The truth that served the sires of old
    The children serves as well.
To every age it may be told,
    And still be sweet to tell.

Its orb-like splendor filled the past,
    And shall the future fill;
For in the mind of God 'twas cast,
    And finished by his will.

Like him, it ever shall endure,
    When time itself expires;
Yea, Lord, thy Word shall stand secure
    'Mid nature's funeral fires.

That Word, then, while the ages roll,
    Shall be our guiding light;
Give hope and gladness to the soul,
    To cheer earth's darkest night.

THE LORD'S MEMORIAL DAY.

All hail! thou gladsome day of days,
   Which saw the great Redeemer rise.
A glorious monument of grace,
   Thou tellest us of paradise.
We hallow thee for his dear sake
   Who brought salvation from above,
And thy returning visits make
   A fond memorial of his love.

In memory of creation, thus
   We give to rest one day in seven;
While yet to him who rose for us
   The first fruits of the week is given.
And so, replete with good to man,
   Our Sabbaths tell of wonders done,
Creation's and redemption's plan,
   Wrought by the Father and the Son.

THE HOLY DAY.

Hail, holy day! whose hallowed hours
Were given to rest my wearied powers,
To fan the altar-fires of love,
And bear my thoughts to things above.

To-day I turn from earth's affairs,
And lay aside its load of cares,
To sit as an invited guest,
Where Jesus bids me sweetly rest.

My Savior, come and meet with me,
And let my spirit feast with thee,
And in my heart a peace distill,
As dew of Hermon's holy hill.

So shall my earthly Sabbaths prove
A foretaste of the rest above,
Until no more on earth I roam,
But rest and feast with thee at home.

JOY IN WORSHIP.

Again the day of God is here,
    On which we leave our toil and care,
And in our Father's house appear,
    To offer him our praise and prayer.
How bright the holy hours it brings,
Which give a glimpse of heavenly things.

Begone, ye baubles that would turn
    Our thoughts away from him we love!
His presence makes our spirits burn
    With longings for our home above;
For these communings in the breast
Are pledge of our eternal rest.

Oh! better one such hour as this
    Than all the pleasures earth can give.
'Tis here we prove what pleasure is;
    'Tis here we learn the way to live.
Lord, give new blessings here to-day,
As in thy house we praise and pray.

IN THE SANCTUARY.

Gen. xxviii. 17; Ex. iii. 5.

How dreadful is this place,
    With God alone,
When all his wondrous grace
    He maketh known,
As humbly here we bend,
And prayers and praises blend,
Which as perfume ascend
    Before the throne.

O earth! stand thou aside,
    And disappear
Thy care, and pomp, and pride,
    Since God is here.
Our souls—put off your shoes,
And with mute fervor muse,
Lest we his unction lose
    Who draws so near.

The gate of heaven is this,
    Which foretastes brings
Of the unmingled bliss
    Where Gabriel sings.
Lo, here, within the gate,
Our spirits grow elate,
As though we scare need wait
    The gift of wings.

GETHSEMANE.

The God-man is groaning
  In anguish alone,
Unthought of by millions,
  Forgot by his own.
He prays 'mid the silence
  And darkness around,
And sweats till as blood-drops
  It falls to the ground.

Mere mortal has never
  Seen sorrow like his.
Ask, What is it causes
  Such anguish as this?
Oh, blush, guilty spirit,
  And answer with tears,
Thy sins are his burden,
  The sins of thy years.

Oh, surely such pity
  As his can not fail;
And, surely, such anguish
  For thee must prevail.
Then cling to him, trusting
  For pardon and peace,
Who suffered to save thee,
  From sin will release.

THE COSTLY SACRIFICE.

Amazing sight! On Calvary's tree
    A sinless victim dies.
Look up, my wondering soul, and see
    The costly sacrifice.

Heaven's richest gift, the Son of God,
    Is there an offering made;
And, lo! as Justice plies the rod,
    On him thy stripes are laid.

Dear Savior! hast thou done so much
    To rescue me from hell?
And shall not all my life be such
    As proves I love thee well?

O dearest Lord! reproach and pain
    Shall only welcome be;
For I will count it all as gain
    To bear so much for thee.

AN ADVOCATE WITH THE FATHER.
1. John ii. 1.

O thou, my Advocate above,
   Whose wounds provide a cleansing flood,
I cast myself upon thy love,
   And trust the merits of thy blood.
I would present no other plea
Than this, that thou hast died for me.

Thy wounds are eloquent in prayers,
   For all who seek thee in distress.
The Father on his oath declares
   He waits to answer and to bless.
Then reconciled I now may be;
Since thou in heaven dost plead for me.

Thou canst not plead my cause in vain;
   I can not trust thee and be lost;
For God will not my suit disdain,
   With pardon bought at such a cost.
No, now I feel my soul is free,
Since Jesus died and lives for me.

SELF-DENIAL.

All selfishness is sin.
Then self must be denied;
For self can never reign within,
And Jesus there abide.

Content from him alone
Our rules of life to draw,
Our heart must be his humble throne,
His will our only law.

Each temper, passion, lust,
Our reason and our will,
Must own his government as just,
And its behests fulfill.

My Lord, I all resign,
Thy follower to be,
Content to know that thou art mine,
And I am owned of thee.

CONSECRATION.

I bring my heart to thee,
    My heart so full of sin;
Thy grace alone can be
    A cleansing power within.
My hope is all in thee;
Have pity, Lord, on me.

I bring my all to thee.
    Alas! the gift is small;
But more there can not be
    Than just my little all.
Oh, may the gift find thee,
Whose love gave all for me.

I cling, O Christ, to thee;
    My only hope art thou.
Oh, let thy death for me
    Be my salvation now.
Accept my gift to thee,
And give thyself to me.

FAITH.

Faith is the eye that looks above,
    When all is dark below,
And finds in God's unfailing love
    A solace for our woe.

When, in the soul's triumphant hour,
    We feel salvation nigh,
Faith is the power that brings the power
    Of blessing from on high.

Faith is the head of weakness laid
    On an Almighty breast,
Where hell can never make afraid,
    Nor earth disturb our rest.

When on the verge of death we stand,
    And life's last link is riven,
Faith is the hand that grasps the hand
    Which lifts us up to heaven.

DESIRE FOR FAITH.

I want the faith that will not fear
    To go where God shall guide;
That has for him an ear to hear,
    While walking by his side.

I want the faith whose fingers brace
    His will in each event;
That in the mysteries of his grace
    Interprets the intent.

I want the faith that dares to trust
    Whene'er it can not see;
That turns to him and says he must
    Forever faithful be.

Oh, may this faith be firm in me,
    So long as I have breath,
Through all my life God's hand to see,
    And grasp that hand in death.

SELF-RIGHTEOUSNESS VAIN.

Shall I, whose sins are mountain high,
    Whose heart is vile within,
Attempt by righteousness to buy
    Salvation from my sin?

Can I to holiness attain,
    While sin is what I love,
And cleanse my heart from inward stain
    Till fit for heaven above?

Nay, Lord, I have no righteousness
    On which to build a hope,
No power of native holiness
    With such a heart to cope.

I need atonement for my sin;
    But I can not atone.
I need almighty power within,
    Or useless is my own.

My only refuge, Lord, art thou,
    To save me from despair;
Low at the cross my soul shall bow
    And find salvation there.

SAVED BY GRACE.

I thank thee, Father, for the grace
  That turned my steps to thee;
For I had never sought thy face
  If thou hadst not sought me.

The condescension of thy love
  My wayward feet pursued;
Turned first my thoughts to things above,
  And then my will subdued.

Thy grace has kept me in the way
  That I so long have trod;
And still it draws me, day by day,
  More close to thee, my God.

Now, after all thy mercies past,
  I can but trust in thee,
To bring me safely home at last,
  Thy presence there to see.

ASSURANCE.

I know I am saved by the blood of the Lamb,
 For the promise to sinners is given,
That he who believes and the Savior receives
 Doth enter the kingdom of heaven.

I know I am saved by the blood of the Lamb,
 For the Spirit now whispers within,
The witness to give that in Jesus I live,
 Set free from the bondage of sin.

I know I am saved by the blood of the Lamb,
 For evil no longer I love;
My heart is on fire with a holy desire
 For good that descends from above.

I know I am saved by the blood of the Lamb,
 For the love of the Savior is mine.
I am saved by his grace, and I feel the embrace
 Of a power that is surely divine.

MY TRUST.

II. Tim. i. 12.

I know him whom I have believed,
    And still I dare believe
That since he has my wants relieved,
    He ever will relieve.

I know not what before me lies;
    Nor do I care to know.
Enough that he is good and wise
    Who guides me where I go.

For while enfolded in his care
    I fear no threatening ill;
His goodness my lot prepare,
    His wisdom lead me still.

That goodness will my steps attend
    Through all life's devious way;
That wisdom bring me, in the end,
    To everlasting day.

GRACE FOR GRACE.
John i. 16.

The grace was great that first I knew,
By which my heart the Savior drew
    With cords of love divine.
My former fears it sweetly stilled,
And with new hopes my spirit filled,
    When heavenly peace was mine.

But 'mid the scenes of stormy strife,
And labors of my later life,
    A greater grace is given;
A grace to stand the stress and strain
Of trial, trouble, toil and pain,
    Where other hearts are riven.

And of his fullness all receive
Who truly on the Lord believe,
    In daily growing grace.
So shall it be till life is past,
And glory crowns us all at last,
    As we behold his face.

SEEKING HELP.

When my soul is weak and weary,
    Take me, Father, by the hand.
When my path seems dark and dreary,
    Lead me toward the better land;
        There to praise thee
    With the glad immortal band.

In the desert be my Fountain;
    In the darkness be my Light;
When in danger be my Mountain;
    When in weakness be my Might;
        In all trouble
    Be my Solace and Delight.

When I pass the shadowed valley,
    Let thy presence light the place;
In a last victorious rally
    Give to me triumphant grace,
        Till in glory
    I shall see thee face to face.

FREE IN CHRIST.

No more a slave in Satan's power,
    By lusts and passions bound,
I am a freeman since the hour
    When I the Savior found.

The blood for me on Calvary spilt,
    Atoning for my sin,
Has freed me from the sense of guilt
    That burdened me within.

I saw in him my substitute,
    Whose merits are divine,
And he those merits did impute,
    As though they all were mine.

Then came the Spirit's gracious power,
    And power to me he gave;
So, ever since that blessed hour,
    I am no more a slave.

GLORYING IN CHRIST.

Gal. vi. 14.

God forbid that I should glory,
  Save in Jesus crucified.
'Tis my joy to tell the story
  That for me he lived and died.

Human love can find no plummet
  That can sound the depth of his;
Human thought attain no summit
  Whence to see how vast it is.

Oh, the wondrous joy of loving
  One who has such love for me!
Oh, the privilege of proving
  That my heart can thankful be!

Ever shall it be my glory
  To extol the crucified;
Ever would I tell the story
  That for me he lived and died.

THE SINNER'S FRIEND.

Long my laboring soul had toiled
  On a darksome sea of doubt;
Waves of anguish, bursting wild,
  Tost my helpless bark about.

Then I saw a wondrous form,
  As I gazed with wistful eye;
Jesus spake amid the storm:
  "Fear not, sinner; it is I."

Then he bade the tempest cease,
  Lulled the billows into rest;
When I felt a holy peace
  Sweetly stealing through my breast.

Now, my Savior, stay with me
  Till I gain the farther shore;
For if thou my guide shalt be,
  I am safe forevermore.

THE HEAVENLY BREAD.

John vi. 48.

Blessed Jesus, heavenly Bread,
Let me on thyself be fed,
   That thy life may quicken mine,
   Making so my life divine.
Be to me the living Bread,
As my soul on thee is fed.

Many foes my ruin seek,
And I feel that I am weak;
   Many dangers daily frown;
   Many burdens bear me down.
Be to me the Bread I seek,
Then I shall no more be weak.

Weary with my heart of sin,
Hungry for thy peace within,
   Now my fainting soul restore,
   Let me never hunger more.
Be thou, through this world of sin,
Life, and strength, and peace within.

BURIED WITH CHRIST.

Rom. vi. 4, 5.

O thou, my Savior, crucified
  Upon the cross for me,
I would my passions, lusts and pride
  Were crucified for thee.

Now let the true baptismal shower
  On me be richly shed,
And may it prove its cleansing power,
  Till sin and self be dead.

And let my life be lost in thine,
  With all I have or crave,
Until my soul, by power divine,
  Be buried in thy grave.

Then let me resurrected be
  From all there is below,
And rise triumphantly in thee,
  A purer life to know.

BEARING THE CROSS.

O Lord, the burdens of this life
    Are heavy to be borne;
My soul grows weary of the strife,
    It feels so weak and worn.

And yet no lighter load I ask
    Of trial and of care;
No easier cross my faith to task,
    But grace my cross to bear.

I ask thine arm to be my stay,
    In all I have to do;
Thy providence to point my way;
    Thy strength to bring me through.

So shall I find it joy to share
    A cross of toil for thee,
As thou upon this earth didst bear
    A heavier cross for me.

HELP RECEIVED.

I took my burden to the Lord,
  And laid it at his feet;
When faith soon found a full reward,
  In rest serene and sweet.

For when I laid the burden down
  I calmly left it there,
And found my cross become a crown
  Which was a joy to wear.

So there, in every weary hour,
  Would I my burden lay,
To find that an Almighty power
  Takes all the load away.

PLEASANT WAYS.

In pleasant ways the Lord has led
  My footsteps year by year.
Not that mine eye no tear has shed,
  My heart been free from fear.

But every tear his love has dried,
　　His word my fears dispelled;
And when by fierce temptations tried,
　　His hand my hand has held.

A peace of which the world knows not
　　Has welled within my breast.
Not that no grief has shared my lot,
　　No storm disturbed my rest.

But he has granted me much grace,
　　And been so sweetly nigh,
That I have hid in his embrace
　　Until the storm went by.

Then, bless the Lord, my soul, to-day,
　　For all his mercies past,
And make him still thy staff and stay,
　　To lead thee home at last.

SELF LOST IN GOD.

O Lord, my life, my light, my love,
My help below, my hope above,
Now let thy life be life in me,
That so thy life my life may be.

So like the sun, the source of light,
Thy beams dispel the darkest night;
Then drive the darkness far from me,
Nor leave a cloud 'twixt me and thee.

Inflame my love and let it burn,
That all my thoughts to thee may turn,
And all my love of evil be
Consumed in constant love of thee.

Thus, Lord, my life, my light, my love,
Prepare me for a place above,
Where sin, nor sense, nor self shall be,
But all be lost in love of thee.

GOD MY STRENGTH.

It matters not, O Lord, to me
How great my foes on earth may be;
While thou art mine I shall prevail,
Strong in a strength that can not fail.

Disease may prostrate all my powers,
Or fill my life with languid hours;
But since it leaves thee still the same,
I shall not suffer loss or shame.

Or let the earth to chaos turn,
Ten thousand worlds to ashes burn;
While still on thee my hope is stayed,
My soul looks upward undismayed.

Then let me never look within,
To trust my nature, weak with sin;
But let me trust thy power alone,
Which makes almightiness my own.

AFFLICTIONS.

Lord, I thank thee for afflictions
  That have brought mine eyes to see
Its unnumbered derelictions,
    When my heart was false to thee.
        'Twas a Father
    Laid his hand in love on me.

Not in anger, not in blindness,
  Didst thou measure out my pain,
But in wisest loving kindness,
    For my everlasting gain.
        Now I praise thee
    For the blessings that remain.

May the secrets inly told me,
  In the depth of my distress,
Be so many bands to hold me
    In eternal faithfulness;
        Then thy goodness
    I forevermore will bless.

THE CROSS TWICE BORNE.

I took the cross and thought I must
    Do something for reward;
My soul had but a feeble trust,
    And oft forgot the Lord.

The cross grew heavy, and the road
    Was very hard to tread.
My soul was weary of its load;
    My feet with traveling bled.

I bore the cross, because for me
    My Savior bore the same;
No more a cross it seemed to be,
    But as a crown became.

I felt my strength was now divine;
    My Lord and I were one;
The blessings of the cross were mine;
    The burden—it was gone.

LOVING THE SAVIOR.

My Savior, thou art dear to me,
 The fairest of the fair;
Not heaven itself a heaven would be,
 If thou shouldst not be there.

In vain the things of time and sense
 Would try to rival thee;
Thy love, in its omnipotence,
 Forever keepeth me.

Though flesh is weak and prone to err,
 In thee is strength indeed;
And thou art such a comforter,
 No better do I need.

Then I will love and serve thee still;
 And if I aught deplore,
'Twill be that I have served so ill
 And have not loved thee more.

TRUST IN CHRIST.

In faith I now can take my stand
  Upon the precious promises,
And smile when woes on every hand
  In threatening thunderclouds arise.

What matter though my foes are strong,
  Since Christ is stronger than them all?
Should multitudes around me throng,
  At his rebuke the last must fall.

Let hand in hand for ill combine,
  This I would know, and this alone:
That I am Christ's and Christ is mine;
  For he is sure to keep his own.

My soul would thus serenely rest—
  Without a moment's anxious care—
Upon my dear Redeemer's breast,
  And find its sweetest moments there.

MY TREASURE.

Let others be eager for gold,
    With all it is able to give,
But I have a treasure untold,
    For which it is noble to live.
A treasure eternal is mine;
    A treasure that is not of earth,
Its Giver and Guardian divine,
    And nothing can lessen its worth.

'Twas purchased at infinite cost;
    Conveyed by the Spirit within;
And when I was otherwise lost,
    It gave me salvation from sin.
Then go with your silver and gold
    And perish with them in the dust!
My treasure will never grow old,
    Nor suffer corrosion or rust.

DIVINE GOODNESS.

Had I a thousand hearts to feel
    The goodness of my God;
Had I a thousand tongues to tell
    That goodness all abroad—
A thousand hearts would be too few,
    A thousand tongues too weak,
To feel the gratitude that's due,
    That gratitude to speak.

Unnumbered benefits bestowed
    Unbounded praise demand;
To give a tithe of what is owed
    Would all my life command.
Then how shall I attempt to sing,
    Or how approach his throne?
My heart, my life, my all I bring:
    Lord, take them for thine own.

PRAYER FOR CHRISTLIKENESS.

Lord, teach me how to live for thee
    And lose my life in thine,
That all may see thyself in me,
    And read thy life in mine.

Oh, teach me how to think of thee,
    And help me so to think,
Till thou art as a spring to me,
    At which my soul shall drink.

And let my heart be full of thee,
    As thou art full of love,
That so my one desire may be
    For things that are above.

Take me at last to dwell with thee,
    To gaze upon thy face,
And tell, throughout eternity,
    The glories of thy grace.

PRAYER FOR PURITY.

Most holy God! thy grace impart,
To purge and purify my heart;
And let it be so well refined
That not a sin shall stay behind.

And, oh! may I not only leave
The sins that would the Spirit grieve,
But have thy love so fixed within
That I shall hate the thought of sin.

Help me its hatefulness to see
As it is looked upon by thee;
To hate that hatefulness, and shrink
From it as from destruction's brink.

A DESIRE TO DEPART.

When weary in heart,
I sigh to depart
And be with my Savior above;
For there I would rest,
With none to molest,
And feast on his infinite love.

But when I behold
The labors untold
That fill all his followers' hands,
I can not but feel
Rekindlings of zeal,
To do what his service demands.

Then still I would share
The toil and the care
To build up his kingdom below.
I bow to his will
To labor until
From earth he shall tell me to go.

Oh, help me, dear Lord,
To wait the reward
Laid up for thy servant above.
Yet, when I would pine,
Thou knowest that mine
Is but the impatience of love.

JESUS PRECIOUS IN DEATH.

When life's fast-failing pulse is low
    And death is in mine eye,
With Jesus by my side I know
    It must be sweet to die.
When other friends beside me shed
    The unavailing tear,
This Friend will be about my bed,
    To succor and to cheer.

He knows the path that lies before,
    Though all unknown to me,
And when I reach the farther shore
    His hand in mine will be.
Then let the gathering shadows gloom;
    While Jesus still is nigh,
My faith shall look beyond the tomb
    And find it sweet to die.

SEEKING THE SPIRIT'S AID.

Spirit, source of heavenly light,
Dawn upon my inner sight;
Show the deeper truths to me
That alone I can not see.
Let me view the Savior's face
Till I realize his grace;
Till that grace my spirit move
All its mysteries to prove.

Let me feel a holy fire,
Burning up each base desire;
Rising in a flame of love
Toward the purer things above;
Rising till the world no more
Charms my senses as before,
But the things eternal be
Life's great treasure unto me.

BE THANKFUL.

Look not at the rich and great,
To compare thy low estate,
Lest thy soul should thankless be
For the lowlier gifts to thee.

Rather think of their affairs
As a source of nameless cares;
Cares from which thou art exempt,
With their mighty power to tempt.

Look thou at their poorer fare
Who thy blessings do not share;
That thou mayest not repine
While so much of good is thine.

Think thou of their harder lot,
What thou hast that they have not;
Then thy soul may thankful be
For the good bestowed on thee.

BE NOT ANXIOUS.

Cease, anxious spirit, cease to pine,
    As though thou wert of God forgot;
Think of the blessings that are thine,
    Instead of things that thou hast not.

Though undeserving aught, how much
    Has he apportioned to thy share!
Sure he whose bounty has been such
    Will give thee still a Father's care.

His daily blessings are in store
    For those who daily seek supplies,
And he will give them more and more
    As more are needful in his eyes.

Then count the blessings of the past,
    And here thine ebenezer raise,
Resolved to trust him to the last,
    And he will fill thy heart with praise.

HAVE COURAGE.

Phil. ii. 12, 13.

Courage, Christian, 'mid thy trials!
　Nothing hast thou need to dread,
Though the world may pour the vials
　Of its wrath upon thy head.
Nay, though earth and hell oppose thee,
　Think not thou art left alone.
He who for his service chose thee
　Does not now desert his own.

Think how first the Spirit won thee,
　Working out the Father's will;
Think of daily favors done thee,
　Through the self-same Spirit still.
Onward, then, through tribulation,
　Till his perfect will be done,
Till thou gain the full salvation,
　Till the fadeless crown be won.

WATCH AND PRAY.

O Christian pilgrim! watch and pray
  Against the powers of sin;
A host of foes besets thy way;
  A host assails within.

Watch when the powers of hell are nigh,
  To prey upon thy soul;
Watch when the world would please thine eye,
  To lure thee from thy goal.

Watch when thy heart would lust for sin
  Or welcome whispering doubt.
There's more to fear from foes within
  Than from the foes without.

Then watch, and as thou watchest pray
  To him whose eyes ne'er sleep.
His arm alone can clear thy way;
  His hand alone can keep.

HOLD ON.

O child of God! amid the storm
    That roars around us here,
Be firm and true the dark night through
    Until the day appear.
The clouds of life will yet be past,
    The dawn be bright and clear;
Then raise thine eyes to greet the skies
    Whose dawning must be near.

Hold bravely on; the fiercest gale
    But bears thee o'er the sea;
And though the waves may seem like graves
    About to bury thee,
Have faith in God, who holds the helm,
    And thou shalt guided be,
And anchor cast in port at last,
    From storm and tempest free.

THE CHRISTIAN RACE.

Heb. xii. 7.

O Christian! run the heavenly race
    That God hath set before thee;
A cloud of those who ran before
    To-day is watching o'er thee.

Have patience; they have won the prize,
    In spite of greater trial;
Let them behold thy equal faith
    And dauntless self-denial.

Lay off the weights of worldliness,
    And what would most impede thee;
Then keep thine eye on Jesus fixed,
    And he will surely lead thee.

Behold, he sits enthroned above,
    With eye upon thee ever,
A crown of glory in his hand
    That never fadeth—never.

A FRIEND IN NEED.

Troubled soul, no longer mourn;
On the cross thy sins were borne.
There for thee the blood was spilt
That atones for human guilt.
Now before the Father's throne
Jesus makes thy cause his own;
Watches all the tempter's snares;
Feels the burden of thy cares.

Feeble are thou? Never fear;
Christ thy Shepherd still is near.
Leading thee, from day to day,
In a safe though unseen way;
From the desert, bleak and bare,
Into pastures fresh and fair;
And he will not fail to keep
E'en the weakest of his sheep.

LOSS IS GAIN.

Quiet be thy soul to-day,
  Though a loved one doth depart;
He who gave thee takes away,
  To his home and to his heart.

Mourn not o'er the outer void,
  As the grave of what has been;
Rather count the hours enjoyed,
  Leaving thee so rich within.

Through the evening of life's day
  Look with thankful heart above.
He who gave and takes away,
  So has taught thee how to love.

GONE HOME.

Gone home, to rest where Jesus reigns,
No more to suffer aches and pains,
How sweet at length that rest to find,
And leave the weary flesh behind.

Gone home to that fair world of bliss,
To bear no more the cares of this,
But in reposeful pleasure find
All irksome thoughts left far behind.

Gone home, forevermore to be
In spirit from temptation free,
And in thy Savior's presence find
All earthly conflicts left behind.

Gone home! How glorious is thy state!
While we in turn our summons wait.
Oh, may we all that glory find
Who here to-day are left behind!

REJOICE.

Phil. iv. 4.

Let us rejoice in the God of salvation,
  While we press on to the kingdom above.
We are his children by act of creation;
  We are his children by purchase of love.
He has been with us in every temptation,
  Strengthened and led us, delivered and blest;
And he can help in each new situation,
  Guarding from danger and guiding to rest.

What if the shadows of earth become deeper?
  Brighter keeps beaming the sunshine of God.
Dry, then, thy tears, thou disconsolate weeper,
  Treading the path that the Master has trod.
What, if the path becomes rougher and steeper?
  He will proportionate succor afford.
Never lose heart with so mighty a Keeper;
  Rather press on and rejoice in the Lord.

CONFESSION.

Lord, when we view our hearts aright
    As they are viewed by thee,
We blush to look upon the sight,
    So much of self we see.

Thy Spirit strips our motives bare,
    To show what lurks within;
When, lo! beneath what seemed so fair
    Are subtle forms of sin.

Oh, visit us in gracious might!
    Make this a searching hour;
First grant the gift of clearer sight,
    And then of cleansing power.

Let every screen be torn away,
    Where foes infest the heart;
And let our strength be as our day,
    To make those foes depart.

REVIVE US AGAIN.

Psa. lxxxv. 6.

Oh, wilt thou not revive us, Lord,
    And let us thy salvation see;
Some token of thy love afford,
    That so we may rejoice in thee?

Now open thou our blinded eyes
    The secret obstacle to see,
Which in thy people's pathway lies
    And hinders their approach to thee.

And with the light give will and power,
    Whate'er the secret hindrance be,
To give it up this very hour
    And consecrate it all to thee.

Let morning take the place of night;
    Let power instead of weakness be;
Give Zion bloom instead of blight;
    So shall we all rejoice in thee.

FORGIVE AS WE FORGIVE.

Matt. vi. 12.

Lord, our debts to thee are many
    As the sands beside the sea;
And should'st thou forgive not any
    We could not complain of thee.
But the fountain of thy mercies
    With unfailing fullness flows;
Every day thy love rehearses,
    Every night some favor shows.

When our debts to thee confessing,
    We are ever treated thus,
Shall we, while thy throne addressing,
    Hate who debtors are to us?
Nay, Lord; as we hope for heaven,
    As on earth to thee would live,
We but pray to be forgiven
    As our fellows we forgive.

But so great our nature's weakness,
    From our first forefather's curse,
We to mercy, love and meekness
    Are inherently averse.
Then, O gracious Lord, endue us
    With a spirit so divine
That, whatever men do to us,
    We may show a love like thine.

BY THE RIVERS OF BABYLON.

Psa. cxxxvii. 12.

By Babylon's streams of yore
   Her harps upon the willows hung:
For Judah's heart was bleeding sore
   And Zion's songs were left unsung.

But Judah sought Jehovah's face,
   And then no more her heart was wrung;
She proved the riches of his grace,
   When Zion's songs again were sung.

So, when we sit in silent grief,
   Our harps of happiness unstrung,
In Jesus we may find relief,
   Till songs of joy again are sung.

THE WAYS OF PROVIDENCE.

Deut. xxxii. 11, 12.

As when an eagle stirs her nest
    To make the thorns her eaglets tease,
So often God disturbs our rest
    When we would sit in worldly ease.

She bears them upward on her wings
    To give them heart to venture forth;
And so our Father kindly brings
    Our souls to leave the things of earth.

Then by the Spirit we are led
    To seek the better things above,
Where we the wings of faith may spread
    In heaven's high atmosphere of love.

MURMURING.

How oft our thoughts have turned to heaven,
    To lay our secret murmurs there;
Because our Father has not given
    What we have failed to seek in prayer.

Perhaps we looked upon some good,
    Yet saw his hand that good deny;
At which complainingly we stood
    And dared to ask the reason why.

Thus, by our murmuring unbelief,
    Have we so oft insulted God,
And brought, instead of sweet relief,
    The strokes of his correcting rod.

Oh, let us cease our sinful cry,
    And lay our wants before his feet;
He will not turn away his eye,
    Nor fail to grant us what is meet.

WE KNOW IN PART.

I. Cor. xiii. 9.

The morning star of better things
    Is in our earthly sky,
And every passing moment brings
    The heavenly noontide nigh.

The Sun of Righteousness imparts
    A gleam of holy love,
Which gives assurance to our hearts
    Of brighter bliss above.

And thus we know, though but in part,
    The good heaven keeps in store;
A light of love within the heart,
    Until we long for more.

And more will come, as comes the day,
    Which drives away the night;
Earth's morning star will melt away
    In heaven's effulgent light.

THE NEW JERUSALEM.

The New Jerusalem behold,
    Descended from the skies,
But not in masonry and gold,
    To dazzle human eyes.

Mount Zion in the Gospel stands
    More glorious than before;
Her temple not by human hands,
    Like that which was of yore.

Her walls are now the hearts of men
    Built by the Spirit, where
The bright shekinah shines again,
    And shows that God is there.

There dwell, O Christ of God, until
    Thy glory fills the place;
Make all her stones more hallowed still,
    With sanctifying grace.

Build up Jerusalem, thy church,
    Until the nations see
Her glory from afar, and search
    Within her walls for thee.

SAVED BY HOPE.

Rom. viii. 24.

By faith at first we find the grace
   That makes our guilt remove,
In Christ behold the Father's face,
   His pardoning mercy prove.

There is the ground of all our hope,
   On which we stand secure,
Nor fear with earth and hell to cope,
   Enabled to endure.

Thence, from our faith's divinest height,
   Our future home we view,
And, thrilled with rapture at the sight,
   Our onward way pursue.

'Tis thus the hope of joys to come
   Doth save us, day by day;
It speeds our steps to reach that home,
   And cheers us by the way.

Oh, may our faith grow stronger still,
   And make our hope more bright,
Until we stand on Zion's hill
   In everlasting light.

IN THE WILDERNESS.

From sin's Egyptian bondage free,
In journeying a season, we
   Have Canaan in our view.
A tedious wilderness we tread,
Yet, by our trusty Captain led,
   Our journey we pursue.

That goodly land before us lies,
And we in favored moments rise
   To Pisgah's lofty height:
Whence, by the eye of faith, we glance
Across our journey's last expanse
   And glimpse the glorious sight.

Then let us gird our loins and haste
The plenty of that land to taste,
   Where we no more shall roam.
Our heavenly Joshua leads the way,
And we are nearer every day
   To our eternal home.

THE GLORIOUS HOPE.

How blest are they whose toils are o'er,
Who rest with Jesus evermore!
Forgot is every earthly sigh,
And not a tear bedews their eye.

No thought of things behind molests;
Nor aught before perturbs their breasts.
Faith lends no more her glimmering light,
But ends in everlasting sight.

There in the glory-light they shine,
Where sin mars not the life divine;
And there before the throne adore,
To share that glory evermore.

Then, while with troubles here ye cope,
Oh, smile, ye saints, in glorious hope!
And take this as your Father's way
To make you fit for endless day.

THE ALMIGHTY SHEPHERD.

Great Shepherd of the sheep,
  To thee thy flock is known,
And thou hast will and power to keep
  Whom thou hast made thine own.

Their nature is subdued;
  Thy nature has been given;
And, with thy saving grace endued,
  They now are heirs of heaven.

Their names are in thy book;
  Their souls are in thy care;
Their pathway thou dost overlook,
  And all that path prepare.

If thoughtlessly they stray,
  If here or there they fall,
Thy providence points out the way;
  They hear thy Spirit call.

By erring made more wise,
  By falling taught to stand,
Strong in thy strength again they rise,
  Grasped by thy guiding hand.

Then, how can foes succeed
  Against whom thou dost keep?
Their power the Shepherd's must exceed
  Ere they destroy the sheep.

HEAVEN.

We know not, Lord, what heaven can be,
It so transcends whate'er we see;
And yet we look for blest employ,
And happiness without alloy.

Whate'er can give the spirit rest;
Whate'er can make our being blest;
Whate'er can make us more like thee,
Such we expect that heaven to be.

But here we are content to wait,
Till entering on our blest estate;
For soon shall all thy children know
What none can e'er conceive below.

OUR HOUSE ABOVE.

There is a house not made with hands;
Beyond our mortal sight it stands,
   In glory nought can dim.
There God presides, enthroned in light,
And angels, robed in perfect white,
   Enraptured, worship him.

There, as the Father of our race,
He has prepared a dwelling place
   For all the saints of earth;
And all shall meet as kindred there,
And in the common blessing share
   That gives that life its worth.

No narrow scope of earthly ties
Shall circumscribe their sympathies
   And cramp their love, as here;
But God will so his love reveal
That as himself they all will feel
   In that celestial sphere.

Eternally at home, with nought
To stir in them desire or thought
　　That would the Father grieve,—
One family they so shall dwell,
In bliss too pure for tongue to tell
　　Or mortal to conceive.

IN REMEMBRANCE.

While thy table, Lord, is spread
And we break this blessed bread,
We receive it as the token
Of thy body, bruised and broken.

While the sacred cup we take,
Drink of it for thy dear sake,
We recall our condemnation,
Trust thy blood for our salvation.

Meet with us, O Lord, in power;
Consecrate this precious hour;
May we feel that thou art dearer,
And our home a season nearer.

BEARING CHRIST'S AFFLICTIONS.

Col. i. 24.

Lord Jesus, crowned as Conqueror now,
With radiant glory on thy brow,
 Who once wert in the flesh—
From age to age thy people fill
Thy measure of afflictions still,
 As crucified afresh.

Since their afflictions, Lord, are thine,
Thou dost afford them help divine,
 To suffer all for thee;
And they by whom they are endured
Are by thy word, thy love, assured
 They shall thy glory see.

Then give us patience now to bear,
That thy afflictions we may share
 Without a murmuring word;
And when our present woes are past,
Oh, let us find a place at last
 With thee, our risen Lord.

A TEMPLE OF THE HOLY SPIRIT.

O Holy Spirit! can it be
That thou art templed here in me?
Then let me tremble at the thought,
And use thy temple as I ought.

Let not a lust its altar stain,
Or footprint of the world profane;
But be thy power supreme within,
To cast out every lurking sin.

So for thyself my heart prepare,
And let me hear thee speaking there,
Till through my thoughts the words resound:
"Take off your shoes, 'tis holy ground."

As once the bright shekinah shone,
In me thy presence now make known;
That I may feel, and others see,
That thou art templed here in me.

SPIRITUAL COMMUNION.

A smile can reach the heart,
A frown disturb the soul,
An eyeflash make emotions start,
And through the bosom roll.
Then since our spirits thus
Can other spirits move,
Much more can God, who fashioned us,
His power within us prove.

And since these hidden powers,
While in the flesh, are given,
What blest communion must be ours
When spirits meet in heaven.
Unburdened of the clay,
Which comes between us here,
Our trammels will be torn away
In that celestial sphere.

Oh, rapturous height of bliss
To which we then may soar!
When in the world that follows this
We dwell forevermore.

With God we shall enjoy
More close communion there,
And in his service find employ,
While we his glory share.

THE FRIEND OF THE POOR.

O Jesus, the friend of the poor,
    Whose sympathy proved thee divine,
Who camest thyself to endure
    The lot of the poorest of thine,—
May we, by our sympathy, show
    That we are disciples indeed,
In having, as thou when below,
    The hand of a helper in need.

The poor in the kingdom of God
    Are rich in the treasures unseen,
Although they may wearily plod,
    Despised by the sordid and mean.
Then may we remember thy poor
    With sympathy such as was thine,
And, helping their lot to endure,
    So prove our religion divine.

THE INCREASE OF GOD.

I. Cor. iii. 6.

Let the Church, as God hath taught her,
   From all human vaunting cease.
Paul may plant, Apollos water,
   He it is must give increase.

Not in learning's art to reason,
   Not in labor's fervid zeal,
But the Spirit's gracious season,
   Is the power to save and heal.

In the struggle of the ages—
   Truth with error, right with wrong—
Let her, while the conflict rages,
   Know that he is ever strong.

With her eye to him uplifted,
   Let her faith his presence claim;
Then with power she shall be gifted,—
   Power to conquer in his name.

Hitherto his hand hath brought her,
And his mercies never cease;
Let her plant then, let her water,
He will surely give increase.

DIVINE KNOWLEDGE.

Away, ye doubts, that ask to see
    The things that hidden lie!
Life's deepest mysteries may not be
    Beheld by human eye.

We test not by the touch of sense
    The secrets of the soul,
But have an inward evidence
    Of a divine control.

The Spirit to our spirit speaks
    The mysteries of the skies;
And he who this communion seeks
    Becomes divinely wise.

Then come, O Spirit, speak in us
    What else we can not know;
That we may grow in knowledge thus
    And foretaste heaven below.

STEWARDSHIP.

Luke xvi. 9.

Awhile on earth we need
    The little earth can give;
But not a sordid greed,
    Which can no more than live.
Our bodies live their little day,
Then mingle with the mouldering clay.

Alas, if we have past
    Our time in toil and care,
That leave us at the last
    The victims of despair;
Since, by our blessings here abused,
Before a judgment bar accused!

Lord, help us so to spend
    Our little earthly store
That, when this life shall end
    And earth we need no more,
Our faithful use of what was given
May find our souls more fit for heaven.

USING AS NOT ABUSING.

We thank thee, Lord of earth and heaven,
For every blessing thou hast given;
For all that thou dost daily give
To make it good for us to live.

We thank thee for a vast supply
Of beauteous things, to please the eye;
For flowery vales and verdant hills;
For waving woods and rippling rills.

We thank thee for the scented air;
For music murmuring everywhere;
For all we taste, and all we touch;
So varied, pleasant, and so much.

Lord, help us so thy gifts to use
That we may not those gifts abuse,
Lest we their office so reverse,
And make each blessing prove a curse.

WORLDLY CARES.

How prone we are to magnify
    The little ills of life,
As though there were no Sovereign eye
    Upon earth's petty strife.

We lay our plans as though our all
    Depends on their success;
And if one idol project fall,
    We sigh in deep distress.

And thus we turn our thoughts below
    Who ought to look above,
And fill our hearts with worldly woe,
    Instead of heavenly love.

Lord, let our troubled hearts be calm
    As summer's twilight hour;
Our thoughts of thee a precious balm
    That has a soothing power.

CHILDREN OF A KING.

Rejoice, ye royal race,
Ye children of a King!
Who grants you now his grace
Will you to glory bring.
Then patient to the end endure;
Since your inheritance is sure.

Condemn the pride of earth,
Its empty pomp and praise;
Think of your royal birth,
And walk in royal ways.
Live here below for things above,
In all the royalty of love.

Think how the King of heaven
Has deigned to call you his.
Think of the blessings given,
And all the promises.
Then haste with exultation hence,
To gain your great inheritance.

GOD WILL PROVIDE.

Pilgrims bound heavenward,
    Tempted and tried,
Lean on the mighty Lord
    Whate'er betide.
Long as your faith relies
Fixed on the promises,
Lift up your cheerful eyes;
    God will provide.

If you shall troubles meet
    Too great to bear,
Go to the mercy seat,
    Lay them down there.
Ask him to bear them, then
Take them not up again;
Know that he answers, when
    Called on in prayer.

Sure as on Calvary
    Jesus hath died,
If unto him you flee
    Whate'er betide,

Though 'neath a cloud of woes
While earth and hell oppose,
You shall in peace repose;
God will provide.

BE NOT FEARFUL.

Ye trembling souls, by fears opprest!
    Call now upon the Lord;
To him be every want exprest,
    And he will help afford.

His faithfulness you oft have seen;
    Then why in anguish bow?
His word has never broken been,
    Nor will he break it now.

Your unbelief alone enshrouds
    The brightness of your sky.
Be still and trust him, then the clouds
    Before his breath will fly.

Yea, look to him in confidence
    When threatening woes are nigh;
He says that he will bring you thence,
    And God can never lie.

DISMISSING CARE.

I. Pet. v. 7.

Cast your care upon the Lord;
Boldly take him at his word;
Prove his promises, and so
Let your faith to knowledge grow.

Cast it *all* upon the Lord,
For he can such help afford
As will ease you of the whole,
Resting well the weary soul.

Cast *your care* upon the Lord,
Then he will your faith reward,
Bless as he has others blest,
Antedate your heavenly rest.

Cast your care *upon the Lord*;
He will every help afford,
When no other help is found
In the whole wide world around.

Cast it *now* upon the Lord;
Be with him in sweet accord;
Then you soon shall prove it true
That he careth much for you.

DAILY VICTORY.

When twilight fades around the sky,
And we have laid the burdens by
    That chafed us into pain,
How sweet it is that we can say,
"The burdens we have borne to-day
    Shall not be borne again."

The battle fought may be renewed,
And foes arise that seemed subdued,
    Ere we obtain the crown.
Yet every day some triumph knows,
And every twilight brings repose,
    And lays some burden down.

O fellow soldier! let thine eye
Behold thy Captain in the sky,
    Directing thee by day.
Then, in the calm of every night,
Thy nearing crown shall grow more bright,
    As burnished in the fray.

TO-MORROW.

Lodged, Lord, with thee to-morrow lies,
   It secrets hidden in the bud,
And their unfoldment may surprise
   Us with their evil or their good.

'Tis well the fruitage is concealed,
   Or we should toil with little zest.
'Twere pain to have the ill revealed;
   The good would come not at its best.

The sweets of hope the saint would lose,
   And languish, may be, for the goal;
The sinner mercy's day abuse,
   And forfeit, in the end, his soul.

It is a happy ignorance
   That takes, from out a hidden hand,
The daily dole of Providence,
   And asks no more to understand.

'Tis thus, when trusting, Lord, in thee,
   We walk by faith, and not by sight:
And thus, because we can not see,
   Our darkness is our surest light.

OUR OPPORTUNITY.

One life a mortal lives,
  Then doomed he is to die.
One time for toil the Master gives,
  And fast its moments fly.

Awhile we have a power,
  As that within a seed,
To bloom into a beauteous flower
  And bear the bounteous deed.

Once let our moments pass,
  We vainly are appalled;
In vain we sigh and cry, Alas!—
  They may not be recalled.

The seed has lost its power,
  And has no future sun,
To give unfoldment to the flower
  And let the deed be done.

Lord, help us so to spend
  Our moments ere they fly,
That we may serve our being's end,
  And in fruition die

MY MISSION.

Lord of my life, to thee I owe
    Whatever gives that life its worth.
Nought good I am, or have, or know,
    Except as thou hast given it birth.

Sure not for nought that life was given;
    For nought thy blessings are not sent;
But for the destinies of heaven
    They have some great and grand intent.

Among the multitudes of men
    Thou hast not blindly cast my lot;
Nor has thy providential pen
    Shown merely an unmeaning blot.

A place there is for me to fill,
    A work my hands were made to do;
Then help me, Lord, with ready will,
    My proper mission to pursue.

Give me my Savior's eyes to see;
    His sympathizing heart to feel;
That so my daily life may be
    One act of consecrated zeal.

DO THY WORK.

Rouse thee, brother; life is flitting;
   Spend no time in murdering time;
Deem no labor unbefitting;
   Aught for Jesus is sublime.

While a world of sinners dying
   Daily stands before thy view,
Sit not thou, supinely sighing
   Some stupendous work to do.

Face thy work and calmly view it;
   Yet be not content to view;
Daily, hourly, nobly do it,
   For so much from thee is due.

Work, as though the world's condition
   Could be much improved by thee;
Pray, as though on each petition
   Hung creation's destiny.

WHY STAND YE IDLE?

Matt. xx. 6.

Why stand ye idle all the day
   When God has given you noble powers?
Why let the moments flit away
   And leave a wreck of wasted powers?
A mighty work remains to do,
And he assigns a part to you.

Why stand ye idle all the day
   And leave your Master's work undone?
Your life is wearing fast away,
   With nought, perhaps, for him begun.
Think what your idle hours will cost
When once eternal life is lost.

Why stand ye idle all the day,
   Encumbered with a thousand cares?
From God you turn your heart away,
   Despising him and his affairs.
On trifling things ye waste your time
Who might be doing things sublime.

Why stand ye idle all the day,
  With judgment sweeping swiftly on?
When here your life has passed away,
  What will avail the trifles gone?
Oh, choose his service while you may,
Nor stand ye idle all the day.

THE SINNER'S PLEA.

Guilty, Lord, to thee I fly;
Thou must save me or I die.
This is all the plea I make:
Save me, Lord, for Jesus' sake.

Look not at my life of sin;
Look not at my heart within;
Look at Jesus on the tree,
Then in mercy look on me.

If I could for sin atone,
I would weep, and plead, and groan,
But this only plea I make:
Save me now, for Jesus' sake.

YOUR WORK.

Brothers! there is work to do
That is meant for none but you.
Here a wanderer you can seek,
There a pity you can speak,
Or a message you can tell
As no other can so well.

He who portions out the work
Grants no privilege to shirk.
Not a day but brings its share;
Hence there is no time to spare;
Not a day of useless ease;
Not a day the flesh to please.

Up for Jesus, then, to-day!
Seek some soul that goes astray;
Thus find pleasure more sublime
Than is found in wasting time;
Burnish all your nobler powers
With the wear of busy hours.

THE WORLD FOR JESUS.

Go save the world for Jesus,
    Who bought it with his blood;
Let holy ardor seize us
    To do as Jesus would.
Fear not to face affliction;
    Shrink not from toil and pain;
Nay, smile at crucifixion,
    If we a soul may gain.

Go bring the world to Jesus,
    Who waits to take it in.
Such labor ought to please us,
    Who are redeemed from sin.
Remember how he sought us,
    That we may seek the lost;
Remember how he bought us,
    That we may spare no cost.

Go bring the world to Jesus,
    For millions are astray,
And he, the Master, sees us
    If we the work delay.
Oh, do not dare to dally
    With thoughts of worldly ease,
But rouse we for the rally,
    God's world for God to seize.

AT THE MERCY SEAT.

When with languid hearts we meet,
Coldly at the mercy seat,
Caring little to be there,
What a weariness is prayer!

When we feel our hearts on fire,
Burning with divine desire,
Glad that Christ invites us there,
What a privilege is prayer!

When o'erwhelmed with awe we kneel,
And his real presence feel,—
While communing with him there,
What a luxury is prayer!

Fan, O Lord, the smouldering fire;
Stimulate the dull desire;
Let us feel that thou art there,
When we bend the knee in prayer.

PRAY ON.

Pray on; for God, thy Father, knows
　Thy needs before they are exprest.
Through prayer he would thy heart dispose
　To seek a refuge in his breast.

Pray on; for should thy judgment err,
　Thou mayest be assured of this:
That, as thy heart's interpreter,
　His answer will not be amiss.

Pray on, until thy sense of need
　Shall melt the icy forms of speech,
And bring thy glowing lips to plead
　In faith that has a farther reach.

Pray on, until thy soul is nigh
　To where his presence may be felt;
So shall the treasures of the sky
　To thee with liberal hand be dealt.

Pray on, until the power be thine
　To do the work that he demands;
Filled with an energy divine,
　To thrill thy heart and nerve thy hands.

THE HOUR OF PRAYER.

There is a calm, inspiring hour
Which brings to me a secret power—
A power my daily cross to bear,
And triumph over every care.

There is a sweet, reviving hour,
As welcome as a summer shower,
Whose gracious drops refresh my soul,
And make the streams of gladness roll.

There is a glad, expectant hour,
Which dissipates the clouds that lower,
And opens to my raptured view
A glimpse of heaven's eternal blue.

There is a great, triumphant hour,
When even death shall lose his power;
For I shall find my Savior there,
With thee the precious hour of prayer.

ASKING AMISS.

Alas, O Lord! in ignorance
   To thee we often cry,
When, in thy gracious providence,
   Thou must our prayer deny;
For better to deny thine own,
   However much we sigh,
And give us bread who ask a stone,
   Than with our wish comply.

When thus to thee, in ignorance,
   Petitions are addrest,
The answer of thy providence
   Interprets the request.
Then let us at the mercy seat
   In meek submission rest,
Assured thou answerest as is meet,
   In giving what is best.

THE FAITHFUL ONE.

O Thou, whose eye can see
    Whate'er thy hands have made,
In every need we turn to thee
    And ask thy gracious aid.

Since thou hast deigned to make,
    Thou must be pleased to bless
Thy children who thy promise take
    And walk in trustfulness.

Yea, we have found thy grace
    A never-failing store;
For never have we sought thy face
    Without receiving more.

Then still in thee we trust,
    To have our wants supplied.
Thou hast provided, and thou dost
    And ever wilt provide.

BROTHERLY LOVE.

How blest the sacred bond that makes
  Us one in Christian brotherhood!
And dear the union that awakes
  Desires for one another's good.

No other bond should be so dear,
  No other union close as this,
Which makes us one in Jesus here;
  One in our aims and sympathies.

Nought born of earth should come between
  The hearts that Jesus thus unites;
Nor aught our warm affections wean
  From those in whom our Head delights.

Then let us all our burdens share,
  As we our mutual joys partake.
What we for one another bear
  Is so much done for Jesus' sake.

MAN IMMORTAL.

This life is not a breath,
    And then an empty void.
There is a something after death
    That can not be destroyed.

Yes, cavil as we will,
    And reason as we may,
The soul asserts its being still,
    In spite of all we say.

There is a restless thought,
    Which can not be supprest;
There is a mentor comes unsought
    And speaks within the breast.

It tells us that a spark
    Of being burns within;
That should our sinning make it dark,
    It is not quenched by sin.

The soul shall ever be
    A spark unquenchable;
Its outlook as eternity;
    Its home in heaven or hell.

THE ALL-SEEING EYE.

There is a sleepless eye
That watches all our way;
There is a record in the sky
Of all we do and say.

Our very thoughts are seen;
Our motives all are known;
Those thoughts and motives nought can screen
Before a Judgment throne.

There all will be revealed,
Our secret sins disclosed;
Yea, what we thought the best concealed
May be the most exposed.

So faithful let us be
That, when that day arrives,
We may not blush nor fear to see
The record of our lives.

THE FOOL'S HOPE.

"There is no God," the fool hath said,
    "No God that rules on high";
And yet he feels a guilty dread
    When called upon to die.

He fain would live as sinners live,
    In reckless folly here;
His life to sin and Satan give,
    Then die without a fear.

But none can live as sinners live
    Without a guilty woe.
To whom on earth their life they give,
    To him at last they go.

There is an everlasting God,
    Who made and judges men;
And fools at length will feel his rod,
    And see their folly then.

SOWING AND REAPING.

Gal. vi. 7, 8.

Life is the time, the heart the field,
  Where seeds of character are sown;
And as we sow will be the yield,
  When once the crop is fully grown.

Sow to the flesh, then sin will strike
  Its roots in our affections deep;
And like in time will bear its like,
  When in eternity we reap.

To him whose will subjects the soul,
  Resisting conscience, earth and heaven,
Continuing its usurped control,
  An endless impetus is given.

Not death from nature's law has freed;
  He reaps not wheat who sowed but tares.
By sin corrupted in the seed,
  Corrupt is all the fruit he bears.

Oh, let us to the Spirit sow,
  That we may life eternal reap;
In holiness unceasing grow,
  That we that character may reap.

THE DOWNWARD ROAD.

There is a downward road
That leads to death and hell,
And sinners find the dark abode
Where none but sinners dwell.

Though smiling sins abound,
To lure the soul along,
In them no gladsome peace is found,
To fill the soul with song.

But disappointments mock,
And sickly pleasures cloy;
While fears of death the spirit shock,
And so its peace destroy.

If thinking of the end
Can every pleasure blight,
What must it be in hell to spend
An everlasting night?

DIVINE LONGSUFFERING.

Yet awhile the drunken throng,
Wild with revelry and song,
May with horror fill the night,
And the eyes of day affright.

Yet awhile, with bloody hand,
Crime may riot in the land;
Vice go forth with shameless face,
Glorying in its dark disgrace.

Yet awhile may those at ease
Live themselves alone to please;
Zion's watchmen, on her walls,
Daily drowse while duty calls.

Yet awhile the lifted rod,
Threatening in the hand of God,
May forbear; but woe to all
When that rod in wrath shall fall!

WARNING.

Willful, wayward, wandering soul,
Thou art traveling towards a goal
Where alone the wicked dwell,
In the banishment of hell.

Dreadful doom to dreadful place!
Outcast from the God of grace.
Woe of woes 'twill be to know
That thy deeds have earned thy woe.

God has wooed, is wooing still;
Warned thee of the fruits of ill;
Made thee tremble oft within,
In the presence of thy sin.

By thy conscience thus condemned,
And the law thou hast contemned,
Dreadful must it be to dwell
In the banishment of hell.

THE PASSOVER.

On Egypt, in the hush of night,
The Lord Almighty showed his might,
And with the shadow of his hand
Laid low the firstborn of the land.

But Israel's hosts uninjured stood,
Their doorposts sprinkled with the blood;
For where that symbol was in view,
Its sacred meaning well he knew.

Another solemn night is near,
When death to sinners will appear;
And they shall quail to feel its power,
Like Egypt in that midnight hour.

But all the blood-besprinkled band
Shall go from earth to God's right hand.
Then let us search our hearts with care,
To find the blood of Jesus there.

LOSING THE SOUL.

Could mortal make the world his throne,
And call its treasures all his own,
Its sweets would not be sweet within
While mingled with the gall of sin.

With this brief life the scene would end,
And deep remorse his bosom rend.
Then what a hell his hell would be,
When poor for all eternity!

And yet for less are thousand sold:
Immortals are exchanged for gold.
More than a million worlds in worth
They give to grasp a little earth.

Eternal life is thrown away
For the mere trifles of a day;
A day that has so dark a night
They think of it with dread affright.

Where then the gain by sinners sought?
They forfeit everything for nought;
And only endless years in hell
The story of their loss can tell.

DELAYING.

When Jesus calls, Give me thy heart,
In youth we often say, Depart!
And so we turn our Lord away,
To wait a more convenient day.

Again he calls, in later years,
With pleading voice and tender tears;
But still we think the time unfit,
And feel too busy to submit.

Thus trifling on from day to day,
We grow accustomed to delay;
And so in sin our life is spent,
And death decides ere we repent.

O Savior! do not yet depart;
Plead once again within the heart.
Some soul, perhaps, will humbly bow
And heed thy gracious pleading now.

NO PEACE IN SIN.

O ye who stray from God,
Along the paths of sin!
Your conscience, with chastising rod,
Allows no peace within.

In vain you oft have sought
Some lasting joy to find;
In vain against your conscience fought,
To gain a peace of mind.

In vain to seek again
The peace from which you stray.
'Tis God that giveth peace to men;
'Tis sin that takes away.

Then seek at once his face;
From sin and folly cease;
So shall you taste forgiving grace
And all the joy of peace

CHOOSE.

I. John v. 3.

Come, man, and seek thy God;
His pleasant service choose;
He asks no grievous thing of thee;
Then why shouldst thou refuse?

'Tis thine to heed his call;
From sin and death to flee;
To love and serve as thou canst do,
And be what thou canst be.

'Tis his to save thy soul
And give thee inward strength;
To bring thee as a conqueror through
To heaven, thy home, at length.

Then come and seek his face
In this, his gracious day;
In Jesus find thy sins forgiven,
And walk in wisdom's way.

IN THE STORM.

Lost on the dark tempestuous deep,
    The white waves bursting wild,
The Lord lay wrapt in placid sleep,
    Like an embosomed child.

"Save, Master!" the disciples cry;
    While on the tempest sweeps.
"Peace, peace, be still!" is his reply;
    And then the tempest sleeps.

So, oft, the sinner, conscience-tost,
    In weary anguish weeps,
And, thinking he is almost lost,
    He mourns that mercy sleeps.

But let him leave with Christ his sin,
    And prove his saving power,
He then shall find a peace within
    Unknown until that hour.

REPENTING.

I long have trod the ways of sin,
And vainly sighed for rest within;
In vain have tried my heart to fill
With all the empty husks of ill.

In vain I mingled with the throng,
And joined their laughter and their song;
In these, alas! I could not find
What satisfied the heart and mind.

Since rest in sin there can not be,
My Father, I return to thee.
Oh, do not spurn thy sinful child,
Though undeserving and defiled.

In mercy pardon all my sin,
And save me from its power within;
Then guide me in the narrow way,
And save me in thine awful day.

MAKE A STAND FOR JESUS.

Oh, make a stand for Jesus
    In this, his gracious day;
Yes, make a stand for Jesus
    While now he says you may.
The days and years are passing,
    And all will soon be past!
Then what, ah! what awaits you,
    Should this one prove your last?

Oh, make a stand for Jesus
    Ere comes the stress of life;
Yes, make a stand for Jesus,
    To fit you for the strife.
In living and in dying
    This Helper you will need,
Who, when all others fail you,
    Will prove a Friend indeed.

Oh, make a stand for Jesus,
    Who gave his life for you;
Yes, make a stand for Jesus,
    And let your life be true.
Leave not till some to-morrow
    The duty of to-day,
But make a stand for Jesus
    While now he says you may.

THE REWARD OF SIN IS SURE.

Num. xxxii. 23.

Across the path by sinners trod
Is written, by the hand of God,
A sentence none may safely doubt:
"Be sure thy sin will find thee out."

In vain it were to close the eyes;
In vain the warning to despise;
In vain the scoffer's jibes to share:
That sentence still is flaming there.

'Tis fixed as the eternal throne;
Its truth by buried ages known;
And so shall unborn ages, too,
Find out how fearfully 'tis true.

O wanderer in the downward way!
Heed thou the warning word to-day,
And from thy wanderings turn about
Before thy sin shall find thee out.

THE JUDGMENT DAY.

Day of every day the greatest,
   Day for which all days were made,
On the scroll of time the latest,
   Looked for long and long delayed,—
     At thy coming
   Law and love will be displayed.

Day of joy and day of terror;
   Day of hope and day of fear;
Day of sifting truth and error;
   Day to doom and day to clear,—
     Saint and sinner
   Must before the Judge appear.

Oh, for One, our interest serving,
   Who shall of the Judge procure
Better than our bad deserving,
   Else our endless doom is sure.
     Mighty Savior!
   They who have thee are secure.

www.ingramcontent.com/pod-product-compliance
Lightning Source LLC
Chambersburg PA
CBHW030305170426
43202CB00009B/878